HOW TO LAND A JOB

BRENDA S. EICHELBERGER

The contents of this work, including, but not limited to, the accuracy of events, people, and places depicted; opinions expressed; permission to use previously published materials included; and any advice given or actions advocated are solely the responsibility of the author, who assumes all liability for said work and indemnifies the publisher against any claims stemming from publication of the work.

All Rights Reserved
Copyright © 2022 by Brenda S. Eichelberger

No part of this book may be reproduced or transmitted, downloaded, distributed, reverse engineered, or stored in or introduced into any information storage and retrieval system, in any form or by any means, including photocopying and recording, whether electronic or mechanical, now known or hereinafter invented without permission in writing from the publisher.

Dorrance Publishing Co
585 Alpha Drive
Pittsburgh, PA 15238
Visit our website at *www.dorrancebookstore.com*

ISBN: 978-1-6853-7011-4
eISBN: 978-1-6853-7868-4

TABLE OF CONTENTS

Chapter 1 How to Land a Job 1
   The Application Process 1
   The Resume 7
Chapter 2 Prepare for the Interview 9
Chapter 3 Dress the Part 21
Chapter 5 First Impression is the Key 23
Chapter 6 Initial Interview – Change your Mindset 25
   2nd Interview – Demonstrating Your Skills 27
Chapter 7 The Final Steps 31
Chapter 8 Review all Steps again 33
Chapter 9 It's Your Time to Hone Your Skills 36
Chapter 10 You have Landed the Job 41
Chapter 11 How to Succeed After You Land the Job 45

LANDING A JOB THE FIRST TIME: PREFACE

This book is being dedicated to all of you who had a desire to write a book, but you didn't think that you had the tenacity to move forward to write a book in order to reach the next segment of your career. Perhaps to be considered as an author is one of your lifetime goals. As an author, it would provide you with the credibility in the workforce in order to elevate your career to the next level. Whether you have been in your position for the past five years without a promotion or the last ten-plus years, this book is for you.

DEDICATIONS

I would like to thank some of my social media mentors/coaches that I may not had an opportunity to meet but have inspired me virtually to write a book through their teachings. I give huge accolades and kudos because you were truly an integral part in inspiring me to write a book. I would like to acknowledge all my family, friends, and associates that I have diligently worked tirelessly for by supporting you in your vision and helping you land your dream job.

CHAPTER 1

HOW TO LAND A JOB

The Application Process

The first element in finding or landing a job is the application process. There are primarily two types of jobs that you would submit your application to and they include: the public sector (United States Government) or the private sector, which includes nongovernment positions whereby one works for a private company but is physically located in the government facility. In other words, you are getting paid through the private company, but the government pays a private company via a contract.

When you are filling out the application process you are applying for a job(s) that is commensurate with your skill set. This is the basic process for applying for a job.

Whether, you are applying for a job as an Information Technology Analyst or a Financial Analyst. Engineering, Acquisition, Sales or Cashier at a Retail store etc., in the workforce, this book will be beneficial for you.

If you are new to the workforce, you will fill out an application for a job at a company where you have an interest. If you are interested in a job, you will apply for a job via kiosk or via your personal computer. Usually a Human Resource (HR) person at the job from where it is posted will provide you with the uniform resource locator (URL) address. You can also apply for a job using a search engine site called "Indeed."

The application will include your name, mailing or home address, phone number and email address. The application shall include your social security number and your driver's license number, date of birth, etc., (as required). In today's job market, it is necessary that you are cognizant that this personal identified information (PII) goes directly to the Human Resource Office and there are persons that hold required security clearances to handle these types of sensitive information.

Sensitive information is not shared to other persons that do not have a need to know due to the sensitivity of the PII information. An individual could be charged with civil or criminal crimes; it depends on how the information will be used. As I indicated, your personal information is sensitive, and it is safe. What you should be aware of are hackers that will try to steal your information.

Do not provide your SSN or your social security card to anyone that does not have a need to know unless you are filling out an application. When you submit a resume, none of your PII should go on your "resume."

The main purpose of an application is for employers to enter various applications in their database for future job openings. The company may or may not have an actual job that is available. In other words, if you do not hear anything from an application within a month or six weeks while applying for a private sector job, it is fine to give them a call to discuss your application status. The application will ask you what hours you are available and your potential start date. There is nothing wrong with stating as soon as possible (ASAP) to provide your availability on the application. The application will request for your current pay.

If you are working and have worked on a job for at least five years, I will always advise people to ask for at least 10–20% more than what they are currently making. It is usually safe to ask for 15% more instead of asking for the maximum amount of 20%. As a result, you must keep in mind that you do want the job. You may not ask for the maximum amount because they might want to offer the job to someone else if you exceed the maximum amount and go beyond what you are currently earning.

An application process is usually done online. You do not have to make any first impressions concerning the way you are dressed or how you look because you are not in contact with the HR person that would be doing the hiring. You're only in contact with the hiring officials if you are applying for a retail store position or another service-oriented job that performs a service. In retrospect, there could be a possibility that you may encounter HR professionals that are responsible for hiring you if you are applying at a Job Fair. At these widely attended events, these types of job venues are known for hiring people on the spot.

Another application process is the United States Office of Personnel Management (OPM), the public sector.

The United States Government is the largest employer in the US. You can apply for jobs throughout the US and oversees via USA Jobs.gov. This process has changed significantly over the years and it can be quite complex in filling out the application if this is your first time doing so. Once you register on the website, you are required to remember a code and the USA Job.gov via the OPM system will text you a code. Once you perform a registration process, write it down and do not share this code with anyone. Once you are in the system, you can apply for a wide array of jobs from electricians, border patrol officers, budget analysts, acquisition specialist, lawyers, nurses, engineers, etc.

This voluminous process is ideal, especially if you are living in a major metropolitan area where there are government offices and military facilities that are within proximity of where you live. The job process through OPM could take anywhere from three to eight months in order for someone to call you in for an interview. This requires patience for you to receive potential employment with the government due to the competitiveness of the jobs that are in demand.

This process also includes an elimination process. If you do not answer all the questions on the application process while you are applying for a job, you either get eliminated or lose your chance for employment opportunities. To avoid this, ensure that you have many of the skill sets that are listed in your application and that these skills are identified in your application that you are currently applying. You do not want to overrate yourself, but you do want to rate yourself in a manner that is fair to you where you can be called in for an interview. It is also feasible to read over the entire OPM application process before you start applying for various jobs. If you do not have the experience that the agency is asking for, it is best not to be overly confident that you will get the job because you don't want to set yourself up for failure.

It is better to apply for a job that you really want, and you are interested in rather than to apply for job(s) to gain the experience.

It is not likely that you would receive "on the job" training (OJT) not unless you are new to the workforce with no experience. In this competitive market, you are expecting to come with the knowledge, skills, and abilities. If you want to apply for jobs just to get the experience of interviewing or to improve your probability of landing a job in your field, you can do this just to build up your confidence and go through the drill of actual interviews. This is a way for you to evaluate yourself, and later you can jot down things that you excelled at or to identify where you need to improve your skills.

This process may be okay if you do not need a job immediately, but if you are in urgent need for a job, it's best not to focus too much on sending out applications where you hardly have any skills. I am implying that it is necessary that you send out numerous applications; however, if you are not receiving any feedback from the jobs where you have applied, you might want to change your strategy and ask for help from someone objective to review your resume for clarity, conciseness, and completeness.

It is unnecessary to waste your time and apply for jobs where you know you do not possess all the qualifications that are listed for the particular job(s).

Continue to apply for as many jobs that you possibly can that meet your skill sets.

Whether you are applying for jobs in the public sector or private sector, there is a list called the "best qualified list." If you didn't make the best qualified list, you would not be on a referred list. A referral list does not mean that you have a job. It just means that you have answered all the questions in accordance with the specific duties that are in the job announcement. There is a possibility that you could potentially be considered for the job; hopefully your application will be considered for the selecting official based on the job announcement and based on how well you answered the questions in the application.

If you answered every question to the best of your knowledge and you expounded on how you performed these skills, at this stage, you could expect to receive a phone call asking you to come in for an interview.

In the private sector, sometimes the HR Division may receive approximately 75–80 resumes. There is a probability that there are equal applications that are received from the public sector. It is the responsibility of the HR Division to determine the best applicants or eliminate some of those applications based on the lack of qualifications and then down select the applications based on minimum qualified to the Highly Qualified list or Best Qualified list.

It depends on how many applications are received from the Division. It is a known fact that every person that applies for a job does not qualify or receive an interview. This interview process is sometimes daunting; however, it is the HR's endeavor to down select from the candidates received for a specific job to eliminate biases and to choose the best qualified persons for the job.

Sometimes, there are several positions located throughout the US, and if there is only one position that is available, it is still best to apply for various jobs to ensure that you have been referred and have an opportunity.

If you have been referred, this assures that you are submitting your application properly and you are including pertinent information based on your qualifications.

After this step, you may receive a phone call to physically come in for a job interview or via telephone. Continue to remain steadfast in your job search and don't give up; a job will come if you follow the steps that are listed in this book.

I would like to explain the difference between a contractor job and a government job. Some of the private jobs that are listed give the appearance that you are working for the government; however, you may be working on the government's site.

However, these jobs are labeled as "contractor positions."

Although, the job is advertised as such, you are still considered working for a private company and you may or may not receive all the government holidays. You might be requested to work on some of the government holidays because your company has an HR Division that you must abide by their rules. If you are a seasoned employee, you may already know this.

Prior to my joining the federal government, I did not understand when the government had Holidays and we were not privy to certain ones and I had to drive to work to my private company while I was a contractor in order to receive payment for a Holiday(s).

This is before teleworking became ubiquitously throughout private companies and public. Something else that you might want to consider, please discuss all other questions with your Program Manager (PM) at your company for all other concerns that you may have surrounding Holidays and any other pertinent information that may not be included in your "Employee Handbook." I had to literally drive to my company's worksite if I wanted to get paid for Government Holidays that were not included in my contract.

Therefore, it is important for you to sit down and talk with your PM at your company to obtain knowledge or situational awareness governing all rules and regulations. It is necessary for you to be equipped with the proper knowledge and of the company standards.

Keep in mind that your primary paycheck comes from your company. If you are working onsite at the government's facility, there is a Contracting Officer Representative (COR) that will be a contact person to ask basic questions for emergency purposes. It is still the best policy to contact your PM for all information to ensure that you are successful on the job. While working onsite at the government facility, always present yourself in a professional manner at all times. Integrity goes a long way in your professional life as well in your private life.

If there are jobs that are available for you to apply for and you are eligible, then apply. To find out more about the Federal Pay Scale, which is usually on a general schedule (GS) Pay Scale, you can obtain a current one by going on OPM's website and pull down the pay scale in the region that you are interested. There are usually no restrictions when you are going from private to government. It gets a little complicated when you want to switch from government to a private company and you have worked directly with the private company. I will mention the sensitivity briefly.

Usually, if you have been working in e.g., finance, budget, contracting or other fields and you are offered a job performing the same duties, you are not allowed to accept the position. It might be necessary to recuse yourself from the government for at least a year or two years.

The Resume

The resume is the foundation of landing that job the first time due to the contextual information that the resume should have. Some of the key attributes of a good resume is having all the key elements. If the key items are not listed, it will not have a chance but if you have the key elements in the resume you will succeed. Your resume must stand out from all the rest.

You do not want your resume to fail by not leaving the Human Resources Office and not being moved forward to the Hiring Office.

This process can be daunting as to how your resume goes through this deciphering process, but it is necessary to eliminate the resumes that do not meet the proper criteria to move your resume to the next step. Your resume will get passed on from one office to another office and then a determination will be made as to whether it will get passed on to the Recruiting Office. Once it passes this step, it is sent to the Recruiting Office and that office will decide whether you will get called in for an interview.

Your potential employers receive many resumes daily, so it will help you to make your resume stand out from others.

There are a couple of ways to write a resume by using bullet format or writing it in paragraph format, I personally prefer the latter. The reason why I personally prefer the paragraph format is that in my experience, a paragraph format receives more positive feedback versus a bullet-style resume, but this is based on your individual preference as long as the main information is included.

I have used them both and I have received more positive feedback in the paragraph resume.

Basically, it depends on what is acceptable at the time. I have also reviewed various jobs as a supervisor and the resumes that are in paragraph forms, were usually selected more often than the bulletized resumes. If you decide to use the resume in a bulletized format, ensure that all your skills matching the position you are seeking are identified in the resume. Try to keep your resume one to two pages

CHAPTER 2
PREPARE FOR THE INTERVIEW

It is necessary to prepare for an interview despite what you have been told in the past. I would like for you to focus on basic skills as you prepare for your first interview with your potential employer.

It is necessary to get a fair amount of rest the night before your interview and do not eat anything that would cause an upset stomach. It is important to think positively prior to your actual interview and maintain the same state of mind during the interview process as well. Prior to receiving the phone call asking you to come in for an interview, there are breathing techniques that you may want to practice. Take deep breaths in and exhale to relax yourself. If you are not a semi or professional speaker, it is imperative that you record yourself using your iPhone or any other recording device. This will help you get used to hearing yourself speak. Once you listen to an actual recording, you may or may not like what you are hearing.

If you don't like what you are hearing, it is essential that you practice two to three times or more per day with a recording device. If you have extra amount of funds, please invest in taking a speech class at your local community college or university.

Another alternative is to hire a speech coach. If Ms. Oprah Winfrey had to hire a speech coach, I am sure you would highly benefit from one as well. She felt as though she needed a coach and it is obvious how it worked out for her because now everybody knows that she is not only an avid speaker/philanthropist, and billionaire today.

Former President Bill Clinton is also an avid speaker and he has spoken at various schools/colleges and universities. Former President Barack Obama and Michelle Obama are also avid speakers.

Also, listen to your favorite news reporters that work for CNN and CSNBC or anybody else that you admire. They all had to take public speaking classes or had a coach that taught them everything that they know today.

Although your job may not necessarily require you to be a speaker, you can also attend your local Toastmasters' meetings. These meetings are offered in various states, and perhaps at a place that is near you.

They are also offered at various non-credit community colleges and local groups. Some of them are offered at your place of employment or a friend's place of employment. The meetings will help you with your growth as you progress from one level to the next.

Sometimes your geographical area where you live or where you have made your permanent residence can be a hindrance in landing a job in order for you to elevate to the next level. This is primarily the reason why some employers do not want to hire persons that have strong accents from various geographical regions.

Sometimes there could be minor language barriers that could cause you to be at a disadvantage when you first enter the office of your future employer. Always be cognizant of how you speak.

There are no 100% perfect speakers that are born; all of us must work on pronunciation and enunciation at some point in our career.

If you have any type of impediment that could possibly be improved and enable you to speak more clearly and fluently, do your best to improve. Perhaps you might ask friends, family or ask a professional coach about how he/she could advise you about how to improve your speech. You would be glad that you did something valuable to enhance your career.

After all, we are judged by our physical appearance, what we say and how well you articulate. Always remember, the more you practice, the more your speech will become perfect. This could be said about people who were born in the United States and those that were born outside the United States. If you have mediocre language barriers, it could prevent you from "Landing the Job" the first time.

Also, try your best to avoid slang language while you are in an interview. Even if the panel is speaking a certain style of slang. Use your best judgment by using correct standard language. Slang language projects an impression that you are uneducated, although this is quite the opposite.

It is necessary to remain on the best qualified list by following some of these rules: the proposed company is ranking you on various characteristics—such as if you forget a question, communication skills, e.g., how well are your words flowing out of your mouth.

Realistically, do not let your guard down too much, remember this is an interview and no one has offered you a job yet.

In the interviewing process, the panel that will be potentially interviewing you may ask you a question after they have finished interviewing you.

A question that may be asked, **"If you were offered the position, do you feel more comfortable in working with a team or by yourself?"** When they ask you this question, or a similar question, you might give the panel a potential answer, e.g., "I enjoy working with a team because it gives me the opportunity and the latitude to bounce ideas off with other team members. If I had to work by myself, I don't have a problem leading a team by myself and implementing work on my own. If I am unsure of what I need to provide, I am not afraid to ask questions to ensure that I am headed in the right direction as it relates to the project given."

One would have to be a quick thinker about this question. If you are telling the employer that it doesn't matter. However, you would want to give the panel members something to think about. More than likely, the panel would not offer you a job if you are not articulating well in an interview and you are only using short sentences. Expound on the questions that you are presented. Provide them with examples of how you work well with a group. This is actually a sample of how well you are communicating during this interviewing process. I would continue to behave in a professional manner. Once you get the job, feel free to use slang if it is deemed appropriate to use. Some races are genetically stereotyped; in order to avoid these stereotypes, continue to be steadfast by using standard English that you have learned in school, college, and beyond and you should not encounter this problem.

I would like to reiterate it is necessary to always behave in a professional manner, just like when you land the job, you might have to wait six months or up to three years until you have surpassed the preliminary probationary period.

This time is usually allowed when you first join the company; however, it could also be for a job where you have received a promotion. If you received a promotion, this is a method of how the employer wants to identify how well you are currently performing on the job as well as how you work with others and how you deal with stress.

During this period, is when an employer evaluates your performance to make sure that you are equipped with the proper skills to perform your job as well as to determine how well you fit in with your new working environment, how fast you are catching on with the new processes. If you do not pass this period, the employer reserves the right to terminate you based on above.

Consequently, if you are performing your job and your supervisor has not had any conversations with you regarding your performance that he/she has not advised you that you are not performing, you are in the clear.

However, when the time has come, for your supervisor to evaluate you, he/she might want you to schedule a time that you meet with your supervisor. Considering that you have been in the position for a while, it is fine to ask for feedback as it relates to how well you are performing and what you can do to improve.

On the opposite side of the spectrum, if you are non-performing on the job, your supervisor should have contacted you as it relates to what you haven't been doing. You should be able to identify how well you have been performing or not performing. If your supervisor has not told you that you have done a good job on being timely with tasks or several projects, then you should know what category you are in. (Whether you have performed your work admirably or was late on every task or deliverable.)

In order to be in this status, as I mentioned earlier, you have surpassed this level and you have completed the probationary period.

Companies are surveying your social media pages, to find out more information about you so that they can gauge what type of employee you are and to ensure that you are not involved in any activities that would place the company in an unfavorable position as it relates to the job. Also, most employers are asking for Top Secret Clearances and drug tests before you are hired.

I would like to reiterate—always dress professionally and present yourself professionally; try to have a smile or semi-smile on your face. With a personality like this, you can always capture the interviewer or panel's approval.

Even if you are not the smartest person or the most highly skilled person, it is a high probability that you will get the job that you were called in for an interview. You must learn how to relax before you are called before the panel. This leads up to the next topic.

What I have found to be helpful, take three to five deep breaths before you are called in for the interview. This exercise is handled so discreetly, no one will ever see that you are doing this exercise. Another suggestion is to have a sincere smile on your face and try to smile with your eyes. This simple exercise of taking deep breaths and holding them and releasing very slowly, will help eliminate any nervousness or anxiety that you are having.

I will let this marinate in your mind for a few minutes because your smile should be sincere and honest. There is nothing more unpleasing than to come into the employer's office with a "cheesy smile" that is not genuine. I'm sure you have been told to "Be Yourself."

Sometimes people may smile, and it is not with their eyes. You really want to practice this in front of a mirror if possible or with your phone.

Have you ever noticed that some people just have a big smile on his/her face and their eyes fail to project what they want you to see?

You introduce yourself, shake everybody's hands— if it is appropriate to shake hands; since the pandemic is prevalent, you may give a nod or an elbow bump—and let them know you are pleased to meet them and say something like, *"Thank you for taking time out of your busy schedule to meet with me,"* or *"I am grateful that you took the time to meet with me on this job opportunity."* Think of something very brief. Keep this interview very professional. Answer each question to the best of your ability and knowledge without using "Uh" after each word. Think of potential questions that you think the interviewer or panel would ask you.

Certainly, if you have the experience in the job, you should have some idea how to handle each question that is given to you. If you just couldn't get the question down in your mind, just ask them, "Would you mind repeating that question, please?"

Also use please, that shows respect or manners, another attribute that may catapult your knowledge, skills, personality to the level of getting the job that you applied for by helping you get noticed.

When I say getting noticed, you don't want them to remember you as Tiffany, a proposed interviewee that was not dressed professionally. She had a nice personality, her resume was superb, but if she has green hair today on her interview, she might have purple and green hair tomorrow.

This dress may not be a problem when working at your local art gallery, coffee shop, or any other store where there is no concern about how you look. If you are applying and interviewing for a corporate job, it is appropriate to dress the part.

Once the panel has interviewed everyone for the job, they will have to eliminate from the people they have met by ranking them and scoring them based on the interview. Here is a typical scenario.

If there were two or three interviewees that were superb and the other two were equally qualified to do the job.

They may have to meet with other customers in the organization in order to gain more knowledge of what the job entails, e.g., they would be coordinating with senior managers; working on high-profile projects with high visibility and all three interviewees were highly qualified because they possessed these qualifications. You might assume that if the panel needed two candidates, you are highly likely to be considered, right? Yes, you are correct. Let me use a different scenario—you recall

Tiffany with the green hair, the one that was very articulate with her speech, however, she had the most impressive resume that stood out from most of the other ones.

Remember, she is applying for a business executive position that would allow her to travel extensively and meet with high profile customers or clients that are located within the United States as well as outside the U.S. primarily on the Eastern part of the country. In this position, she would be representing the company. A company has the right to hire whomever they please. That is partly true.

What Tiffany failed to realize is that she would be meeting with various clients within the United States and some clients that are located outside the United States. You are probably thinking that this is discriminatory, but it is not.

The proposed company has already indicated to her that Tiffany would have to meet with senior level management staff. Everybody in the meeting was dressed extremely posh with business attire. If this had been on a telephone interview, perhaps, Tiffany would have had an opportunity to receive a job offer. However, there were other elements that were blatantly obvious that could have prevented this from happening and she could have easily landed an offer.

Tiffany was aware of the difference between a business high profile professional job. However, she was not in tune when she had to travel outside the US, including Middle Eastern parts of the country where the culture for women is significantly different.

If she were offered the position, she would be traveling to various countries and conversing with an array of clients—some located in countries that still have dogmatic ways about how women should be dressed. For example, in some of the Middle Eastern countries, a woman is still required to cover her hair. In this position, she would have periodic dealings with the clients. She possessed all the skills, but this isn't just a regular job where there would be little interaction with the customer.

All these qualities were explained to her prior to the interview process. After all, this highly visible profile management staff would cause her to travel to conservative places.

Green, purple, pink hair is appropriate in the US, but other countries might find this dress attire to be unacceptable to a company such as this. This would be acceptable if the position was available in other fields but not for a company such as this. It is appropriate and it would not be an impediment e.g., Art Museum, Tattoo Shop, Lounge, Yahoo, etc. Hopefully, this would be a valuable lesson learned for Tiffany or anyone else that would find him or herself in a similar situation.

It is recommended she become more cognizant of her clothing and appearance for jobs in the future. What Tiffany could have learned from this situation, is to go by the office, if possible, to determine how employees exiting the building look to grasp a sense of how to dress at a company.

This will give one an indication of how to dress appropriately for the interview at the company. It doesn't matter if you put on a suit and you look professional. If you see some of the people coming out of the building or company and their hair is not green, pink or some variation, a person might assume that this is not acceptable for the company's standards or dressed in extremely tight clothing.

This would have given her a typical day as to how they dress at the office where she has the interview. Try not to go on a Friday because on Fridays most businesses allow the workforce to "dress down." The best day to try to do a "dry run" at the company would be Monday through Thursday.

Perhaps you may have access to the entrance to the building and somehow you could strike up a conversation with the office manager that sits at the front desk or perhaps the security guard.

At the end of the interview the persons on the panel will ask you if you have any questions for them. You better have those questions already prepared in your mind what you are going to ask.

Always be prepared to ask the panel at least three questions. By asking them questions that are relevant to what you expect to do on the actual job is key to your success of being offered a job or being called in for a second interview if applicable.

Some proposed questions that you should ask the panel and some that you should not ask:

"Don't Ask" Questions:

Do not ask if you can telework. Do not ask any questions about how many smoke breaks the firm or agency allows.

a. (You can pose the telework question) Do you offer flexibility in working hours and teleworking from home as necessary?

Am I allowed to bring my children to work if my babysitter is ill?

"Do ask" Questions:

Do you offer work balance opportunities?"

Is parking available for everyone or do you have to be at a senior level management position to park in the garage?

Do you offer paid tuition when classes are relevant to your current job?

How would you describe the work environment here? Is diversity a part of the office?

How is the office space arranged? For example, are cubes primarily used or private offices?

Will I be working in a team atmosphere, like an Integrated Product Team (IPT) or alone?

How many people will I be working with or how many people will I be supervising? (if you are applying for a supervisory position)

What are the current Operating Systems that you use here, e.g., Microsoft Word, Outlook, or another system?

Is there an administrative person that will be helping me with setting calendar appointments, meeting space, etc.?

I traveled in my last job and I enjoyed it. Is there travel involved in this position?

For example, I will take the Wellness question above: "Are Health and Wellness breaks allowed during working hours?" Someone on the panel may say something similar. "Absolutely! We offer Wellness." This allows a chance for you to exercise during your regular day and we also provide 1–2 hours per week do this. You will not have to use your annual leave—we have administrative leave that is available for you.

We offer Telework twice per week and this gives you the opportunity of sleeping in an hour because you don't have to physically commute to work every day; we do require you to be available at all times by being accessible to all the normal meetings that we have and dial in for your meetings on your calendar in order to meet with your customers or clients. Primarily, telework should appear seamless when you are not physically in the office.

Don't ask about lunch hours. (The company/agency requires you to take two fifteen-minute breaks or one-hour lunch breaks including your two fifteen-minute breaks. Failure to offer employees lunch breaks is against the Labor Laws and companies or government agencies could be held legally responsible for not allowing employees breaks after working a certain number of hours.

If you are not familiar with the Labor Laws, read up on them at your leisure in order to become abreast about your rights in the workplace. If you are just starting your career, or if this is your second or third career, laws are constantly changing, and it is a good idea to be up to date with the laws.

Let's get started by being prepared for some of the potential questions that you may be asked from a potential employer. Some of the questions would look something like this.

Potential Questions:

What do you have to offer for the company, ABC, Incorporated?

Your answer would be something like this:

My skills are identified in my resume, which states that I graduated from Yale with a 3.8 GPA. I served on various boards and I believe my educational credentials would be an added asset to your organization. I passed the Bar Exam on my first attempt. I am a quick learner, I am an A-type personality, and I am not afraid of hard work. I will bring to the table my organizational skills that I learned in engineering and my leadership skills. I am confident that I have the skill sets and the tenacity to lead this company into the future.

I am still relatively young (under 40) and I can bring other like-minded people in the organization in order to grow the business and to ensure the company's mission is accomplished expeditiously.

We have a diversified staff here at ABC, Incorporated, how well do you understand employees with a diverse background and what you would do to boost the morale in the office?

I believe in treating everybody equally and fairly. We all must be cognizant that the people with diverse backgrounds have had various struggles in life. I would ensure that they can obtain the same training as others in order to be on the same level, especially if they are currently feeling as if they are disadvantaged. I would talk with them by letting them know that all of us are welcome here and if they are dealing with any personal issues, I would try to gain their trust and have a listening ear as necessary.

Where do you visualize your place in ABC, Incorporated within five years or ten years from now?

I visualize myself as a personal motivator to my staff. I try to encourage them to be the best that they can be. I consistently encourage my staff that they should be applying for jobs if you have not moved up when you initially started a job.

An individual should stay on one job for at least two years. By the time you have the experience in a job for at least five years, it is time to elevate yourself. I plan to move from my current job as a first line manager to a second line manager or as a director.

Get Rid of Anxiety by Using Breathing Techniques

Roll your head forward, then gently swing your head from side to side. Stretch the front of your neck and stick your lower jaw out (so that your bottom teeth are in front of your top teeth). Tip your head back and reach toward the ceiling with your chin. Hold for three breaths. Now reach your chin toward the left side of the ceiling. Hold for one breath. Now aim your chin toward the right side of the ceiling. Hold for one breath. Return to center.

To stretch the sides of our neck, wrap your left arm up and over the top of your head so that your left palm is touching your right ear. Let the weight of your arm Tilt your head to the left as far as you can to remain comfortable and feel the stretch on the right side of your neck. Reach down to the ground with your right fingertips so that your right shoulder lowers. Hold for three breaths. Leave your head where it is, let your hands relax and let your head gently float back to center. Repeat on the other side, i.e., right palm over left ear.

To stretch the back of neck, clasp your fingers together in front of you, drop your chin down to your chest, and bring your hands around to the crown of your head. Let the weight of your hands and arms deepen the stretch. Make sure your knees are unlocked. You might feel a stretch down your back as well. Hold for three breaths. (see more of these exercises in *The Voice Book*, by Kate DeVore and Starr Cookman or you can find a plethora of similar books at your local library or take advantage of various research tools through the internet that are available.)

What is considered professional dress today when most offices are casual? There is a difference between applying for a job and having an actual interview.

If you are a female, professional dress would consist of a skirt, blouse, or top in neutral tones or a pantsuit, e.g., gray, medium blue, navy blue or tan with matching shoes and a neutral-colored bag. You can also use a pop of color such as bright blouse with neutral colors.

You may carry a small portfolio including a lined paper writing tablet. This also should be in a neutral color. The purpose of this portfolio is when the panel asks you questions in the interview, you will have something to take notes if you forget a question. You will be prepared to ask the panel a question if you didn't capture the complete question the panel is asking you.

When the panel ask you the question, it is appropriate to pause briefly if you are trying to think of the proper way you want to begin responding. If you do not know the answer right away, ask them, "May I come back to that question?" More than likely, they will not have a problem coming back to a question. The panel realizes that being on an interview is somewhat daunting and most panel members have empathy for you because they have been in similar situations.

The main thing to remember—do not go into to the interview and say you are nervous. That is why it is paramount to take deep breaths prior to entering the room to relax for the interview.

CHAPTER 3
DRESS THE PART

For the male, you should always wear a shirt with matching tie and a pair or dress pants in grey or tan. If you have a suit, wear a suit for business attire. For business casual, you may be able to get by with just a shirt and tie. Always have a fresh-looking suit that is free from wrinkles, spots, and odor, the same would apply for women. Please spot-check your wardrobe before you walk out of your house and check your apparel several days ahead of the actual interview to allow plenty of time to get your clothes professionally cleaned. Another main item to check is to ensure that your shoes are not scuffed.

Your goal is to give a great first impression. After all, everybody that will be interviewing is on the same plane level until you enter the room to sit down and meet with the panel members. You may not know right away if one of the panel members might be your potential managers until he/she states that he is hiring someone to work in his/her department.

Appearance shouldn't be the only standard that you will be evaluated; however, it is the only visible element that the panel can make an assessment before you open your mouth. If you recall previously where I talked about the breathing techniques; be sure to repeat these exercises so that you can be ready to "Land that Job."

I would like to add, if you live on the West Coast, the dress codes are much more relaxed, and it is not feasible to wear a suit. For example, working in an environment such as Yahoo and Google where the office environment is primarily casual. Many of the personnel may wear a pair of casual pants and a blue shirt.

If you are interviewing for a company such as this, you would wear a pair of casual pants and a button-down shirt. Once you are hired for the job, your employer would tell you what the dress code is. If you have written down your homework in advance, you might find yourself taking a stroll at your potential employer on a Monday, Tuesday, or Thursday so that you can get an idea of the dress style or culture.

It would be advisable to do this so that you can survey the office environment or culture. This would give you a heads-up and it would provide you with some additional information so that you could make a prudent decision whether this environment is good for you.

If a company is comprised of men or women that are of a specific group or consists of specific diversity makeup and the company does not offer a variety of diversity and you thrive in being around people that are in that group, you may have to Rethink this particular job offer.

Although in accordance to state laws, most companies that have a certain number of employees are required by law to hire a certain number of persons from diversified backgrounds and nationalities.

If you would like to know more about diversity, you can research this for further information on Google or any other search engines to find out more laws regarding hiring practices.

CHAPTER 5

FIRST IMPRESSIONS

First impressions are the key to standing out from all the rest; it is necessary because you want to stand out to your potential employer by giving them something to remember you. For instance, you can make your resume more impressive by including various fonts and colors in your resume.

You want the person(s) that will be interviewing you to remember your name in the interview; however, whether it is something with your earrings, apparel, or a small icebreaker—something small but memorable to ensure everybody is comfortable in the interview. It could be something subtle but monumental.

For example, if you are in the office and the office has photos on his/her desk of family visiting a familiar place. *You could say that it is a beautiful picture. "My family went there (wherever the location is) a while ago and say something that is familiar.* This conversation could be said for example if you are waiting on another candidate to join the panel.

It would be nice if you (the interviewee could start up a general conversation to break the silence. You want the panel to remember that you were poised during the interview as well as your interview stood out and it was phenomenal. You stood out amongst fifteen other candidates.

You also stood out by answering all the questions that were presented to you and you were completely confident. This is a very impressive stance to be in—second to none. This may be a time to self-congratulate yourself because of the hard work that you have put in the process of applying for the job and being impressive, but don't be overly confident.

On the other side of the spectrum, you did not quite answer the questions that were presented to you and you were not prepared. You didn't read this book and you did not annotate certain portions of this book for you to make your first impression memorable.

You could be thinking to yourself, I should have, could have, would have but you failed to do anything but to go on an interview and you were not equipped with the best skills in order to be considered for the job that you knew that you were qualified to do. I see this quite often when different people in the office know that they are qualified for a particular job but failed to do the proper steps in order to make him/herself more marketable.

That is, they failed to prepare. A saying is: If you Fail to Plan, You Plan to Fail"

CHAPTER 6

INITIAL INTERVIEW: CHANGE YOUR MINDSET

When you are ready to go to your potential employer and interview for a job, the first thing that you need to do is to change your mindset. As soon as you enter the office, your mindset should shift from negative to positive and you should speak over yourself and claim the job that you are applying for is yours. You have already spoken these words to yourself; you have already visualized it in your mind that you are already working in the job. In this scenario, you must relax yourself if you feel as though you are reverting to an insecure self, then you must change your mindset to a self-confidant and self-assured self in your mind. After all, you do have the proper outfit.

You are prepared to give the panel a winning smile (internally and a pleasing look on your face). You can practice until you have a pleasing look and not a big smile. Be careful not to go into the interview with a wide grin on your face. This will not get you the job, and it could be perceived as though your resume does not match what you are projecting in the interview.

I had a candidate that interviewed for a position that I was going to hire on my team. Unfortunately, he did not prepare for the interview. He could hardly answer the questions that we presented to him; however, it was prevalent that he could not articulate what he could perform on the job if the position were offered to him.

After the interview, the entire panel said that he was a nice guy, but he did not answer any of the questions. His background was military, but he lacked the skills for the job, and he did not rehearse for the job interview. If you want the job, you must rehearse for the job. The difference between a smile on your face and a grin is exactly that. Grins are usually artificial, and they are usually on your facial expression the entire time of the interview—actuality, this is not good.

Focus specifically on what you are going to say, and I have already outlined most of those things in the prior chapters. To reiterate, in the interview your clothes are together, no wrinkles and no noticeable spots on your clothing.

Your appearance carries a substantial amount of credence when you are interviewing for a job. You have probably heard this many times, but always give eye contact to everyone that is on the panel and try to give the same attention when you are explaining your skillsets in the interview as you are reading from your resume. Nothing in the interview should take you by surprise; after all the basic criteria that are necessary in an interview is to know what to do, what to wear and what to say.

Research what the company does or what they manufacture, sell, etc., including have a basic knowledge of the mission of the organization and the company.

You may not know the mission of the organization, but you can research that as well. It might give you that upper edge of awareness before the interview in order to be prepared for something about the company including its mission. This could be very brief; however, if you've been researching various companies, and you don't remember, the vision and goals of the agency, it's fine just to have the mission written down on a notebook or portfolio.

You could alphabetize all of these in order by the date and time you are to visit the company by the first to the fourth company that you are interviewing for the same day.

You can create a form in Excel or in whatever format you like. This is for your personal use. You could include who you will be meeting with the time and how long the interview. It is necessary to use time management strategically. You do not want to schedule your interviews too closely apart because some of the interviews will generally go over the scheduled time.

It would be time effective if you could leave at least 1.5 hours between consecutive interviews. For instance, if they are all located in the same area, you should not have any problems meeting this goal. Generally, it is best not to interview more than two per day; however, this should be based on your personal situation.

There could be extenuating circumstances whereby your company is downsizing. In this case you would want to be more aggressive by allowing at least three to four interviews per day in order to alleviate having too many interviews in one day.

As I mentioned before, it is a good idea to place the names in your portfolio so that you can recall what was mentioned in the interview so that you can have some information that would be helpful for you when you receive a second telephone call.

The Second Interview – Project Your Skills

You have made it to this step, and you should be commended to have made it this far. Most people do not make it to this step; however, you have made it and it is really time to project your skills to another level. You must first rethink about what has gotten you to this position. Was it your attire? This is an integral part of pulling this entire interview process together. You had your portfolio and you answered all the questions correctly and if you did not answer them, you would not be in the position of being called in for a second interview.

Whatever you did, you should take some more notes and ask yourself, what could I possibly do in order to catapult to the next level so that I can actually receive a phone call from the company or agency in order to be selected for a position?

The answer to this question is to prepare, prepare and prepare, but do not overly do this to yourself because it is always best to avoid stress. Once the excitement wears off, review your notes that you jotted down in the interview and try your best to recall the most pertinent things that you said in the interview panel or what was the most important thing that they were impressed about you.

All of these are attributes that you could use in the interview in order to hone onto and possibly be used to your advantage in order to land that job.

Once the employer calls you in for a second interview, you should be prepared for the job well in advance. After all, you did get to this point in the interview process. Thoroughly review everything that I have gone over in the earlier portion of the chapter when I talked about breathing techniques. Although, you may have mastered this process in the initial interview, it will be extremely important to go over every aspect of our earlier discussion including your wardrobe. Make sure that you are not selecting the same suit that you've worn in the initial interview. If you do select the same suit, it is not going to matter if you have selected another clean and fresh shirt, blouse etc., to make it more appealing.

Ultimately, this is the last step in the interviewing process; you might want to be more polished in this interview setting or wear the same style of professional clothing that you've selected for the last interview. After all, you will typically not receive a third interview. What you do want to do is practice going through the questions that you were asked in the last interview but they are unlikely to ask you the same questions as your previous interview or second interview but be prepared for the questions to be similar in context.

This time the panel will ask questions such as your performance, how you would handle various scenarios on the job that you will be doing. In other words, the panel would probably ask realistic questions to ensure that they are making the best decision for the company or agency and they do not want to leave anything that they could possibly question in the interview. It depends on the actual job itself, especially if this job is a higher-level position as a professional engineer, Information Technology professional or a senior level management position.

These are some of the proposed questions that the company or agency would want to learn about you.

This is a senior level position; how would you go about assigning workload to various persons that are under you? (*This question is somewhat vague, so first you would query the skill sets of the team members that are under your management to determine what each level's workload is in order to make a sound decision. At any job, everybody does not have the same workload. Each person works on various levels. Once you find out some of the things about your proposed team, you could perhaps assign the work to the person that has the least amount of work and based on the team member's familiarity with the work itself.)*

Another proposed question would be: How would you resolve a conflict within team members? This is a basic question that could be answered something like this—I would meet with each person separately in order to make a prudent decision. I would make an assessment on the various statements that I have heard from the individuals, and then bring the two employees together. Once I had formalized a comparative analysis of the conflict and then come up with the root cause to identify the best solution to resolve the conflict.

How would you resolve a schedule conflict within your staff if two of your employees would like to be off at the same time and the work has to be completed during the time they would be out of the office? What would you do as a manager?

This is a difficult situation that would require further consideration. For example, more information is required. Perhaps one person will be out of the office for medical reasons and the other person is just going to be away for some rest and relaxation. (R&R) The employee really needed the R&R because she has been extremely stressed out with other projects and trying to get caught up on her work.

There are a few suggestions that one could make. Perhaps the employee is off for R&R and that individual could significantly reduce her leave by coming back in the office to help with fulfilling the organization's mission.

Don't hesitate to ask another employee that is available to spend some extra hours on a project to help the employee as well as to meet the organization mission or goals. It appears that this could be perceived as a win-win method. The person that is shortening her vacation time away from relaxing, would benefit the mission and management would look at her in a different dimension and give her positive feedback to say that she is indeed a team player. When another opportunity becomes available, this individual may be offered the next available promotion as necessary. This is not to say that she did one thing by shortening her time off to come back to work early, but other key elements are also evaluated in the decision-making process.

These are scenarios that could be occurring daily in any work life situation. You may have to deal with various situations in your current position as a manager or in your future roles and responsibilities that you are currently in now. A lesson learned from this situation—no matter what comes up during a typical day at the office, it is best to be prepared for any situation. In the long run, readjusting your schedule to accommodate someone else who would be out of the office while a project that was very important that had to be completed during the time your co-worker was out of the office. This is an extenuating circumstance that neither one of you could predict. By being flexible one could possibly boost his/her career because of one going above and beyond the cause of duty to change one's schedule that could possibly change your trajectory.

This scenario could have gone differently if the person failed to accommodate for another person's leave. She did not have control of this situation. This person could have been negative about the entire situation and told other people in the office that she refuses to give up her leave that she had earned to readjust for somebody's else's situation, she barely speaks to you in the office.

Instead, this person chose to make this adjustment in her schedule to assist the entire team to ensure it was successful. It would work out for her especially if she were able to complete a project on time ahead of schedule. She and the manager would both win in this scenario.

If the individual was not looked upon in a positive manner, you would become to realize that she accommodated management and the entire mission. She looked upon this situation differently due to her apathy for other individuals to reduce her time off in order to finish a project.

We continue to live in a society whereby everybody is for themselves. It is amazing to see a gesture in the workplace that seems to be slowly disappearing, but it is still happening in today's work environment again.

REVIEW ALL STEPS AGAIN

It is important to review all the skills again that I have mentioned before such as breathing skills, projecting your voice to ensure you are not speaking too loudly or too softly while you are preparing for your actual interview and visualizing yourself at the official interview.

Whether this is the initial interview or the second interview, please take the time the night before to go over these with a friend, relative, or your mentor – you will need someone to evaluate how well you are doing with answering questions pertaining to some of the proposed questions that you may be expected to answer.

Try to eliminate "filter" words such as "Awh, Well, err, Ugh, etc., especially when the questions are presented to you. The person that will be going over these steps should be able to provide you with the proper feedback so that you can land the job wherever you have submitted your resume.

It is still a strategic methodology to go over some of the standard processes that have been widely used for decades. Some of these are: Find out all the significant skills of what the firm or agency do, e.g., what the organization produce, manufacture, or manage; how many other subsidiaries are owned by the company that you are applying.

REVIEW ALL STEPS AGAIN

This could easily be researched using a simple search via Google, Siri, etc. It is recommended that you do this as well because the more knowledge that you have about the company, the probability of you landing a job that you are satisfied with would be increased with your research, knowledge, and skills. One of the key points to take away from this book is to prepare yourself to be the best that you can possibly be.

Remember, it is necessary for you to make dry runs at the office that you will be interviewing. This includes finding exactly where the job interview is to ensure that you are on time, prior to 10 – 15 minutes of your actual interview appointment. It is important to estimate how long it would take you to get there and include additional time due to traffic and other unforeseen gridlocks in traffic. After all, this is just an assessment; take into consideration that your exact interview time will usually be in the morning during rush hour traffic, the middle of the day when people are having lunch, or at the end of the day.

With this knowledge, it is important to be prepared for the worst-case scenario, e.g., accidents, traffic for driving or if you are going via bus or any other type of public transportation, there could be delays. Take additional cautionary measures in order to arrive 15 minutes early by checking traffic problems ahead of time before you leave home, as well as take advantage of various apps that will give you instant traffic jams in advance. When you take advantage of the latest APPS it can easily navigate you to alternative routes which can be a lifesaver.

If you happen to be late, please be courteous and alert your person of contact immediately.

Consequently, some issues are not under your control. In some instances, when you will be considerably late, try to calm down and think positive about the situation. If the traffic issue is a major problem, the panel may have no other choice but to reschedule you for another day—don't take this situation personal, because sometimes in life, it may work out the best for you. This may be a domino effect, because several interviews would have to be rescheduled. The objective has already been met and that you have been called in for an interview; despite extenuating circumstances or impediments that have come up and your interview must be rescheduled.

This is also a good time to practice more on your interviewing skills by going over proposed questions that the panel may ask you or to focus more time in perfecting your skills so that you can be better prepared when you are called in for your interview that was postponed. This is an opportune time to do this so that you can make this the best interview ever so that you can close the gap of the others that have interviewed before you so that you can be on the top best qualified person on the list.

Just think for one second, if you have prepared all that you could for this interview and it has been canceled due to major traffic issues, e.g., there are miles of vehicles that have been stagnated for hours.

By this time your stress level has risen to another level and it depends on the weather especially in the summer, your sweat glands are out of control and your anxiety level is over the top. When the POC notifies you to reschedule, do so kindly. It might be the best thing that you have ever done. After all, you must remain calm in an interview while the panel asks you various questions about the job.

Your mental capacity must be intact as well as focused on the job that you are interviewing for in order to land the job.

Dress according for the interview that you are applying for and if necessary, always look presentable. Another thing to keep in mind, always dress for the job that you don't have. To put this all into perspective, you haven't yet landed the job, but it will happen. Dress professionally all the time on your current job and believe in your mind that you will receive the job, no matter what your beliefs are. This doesn't mean that you try to out dress your manager, you dress how you feel.

If he or she believes that you are doing this, then he/she have internal problems that is unrelated to the job. If he or she dresses in a refined outfit every day, this should not reflect on his work performance.

I knew of a person that I worked with in sales at an exclusive retail store, we all worked a part-time job to go back to school or to save for other financial means. A friend of mine at the time looked good all the time with designer clothes, suits, nice shoes, and where he worked full-time, his manager was on his case and he was given subtle attacks by making comments about his wardrobe style. Well, sometimes, people don't realize it and other people say that he is entitled to wear what he wants to wear since he works hard for his money to purchase the clothes that he wears. I told him that was fine, but it would be beneficial to tone it down because he looks as if he was about to do a photo shoot in a major men's magazine.

Shortly, this individual was terminated and obviously he couldn't use the way he dressed as a method to fire him, but his manager had to come up with malicious tactics to have him fired. This is what I mean, you want to set a very good example, but you do not want to look better than your manager especially if he knows that his subordinates exceed the way he or she dresses. In order words, he lost that job, but he received another offer for another job working for an exclusive well-known hotel chain.

It took him awhile to land another job, but he even found another one with better pay and benefits. Several years later, he said that his current manager always compliments him on his style.

Even though the individual didn't know at the time how much of an impact of how he dressed by wearing designer suits and shoes at his previous job, he wanted to dress the way he wanted despite the snide remarks that he received from his manager. Some people are insecure, and his manager felt as if my friend could not dress better than he could.

There are some huge benefits in working for an upscale department store. We received 20% discounts for employee discounts plus an additional 20% off on all sale prices. We were working this part time job to supplement our incomes while saving for other large item purchases that we wanted as well as to look good on our full-time jobs by having extra money to buy high quality designer clothes without paying full price.

My friend did not do anything wrong; sometimes it's the perception of how some managers perceive subordinates.

His manager did not feel as though someone like him who is not in a management position could afford to dress the way he was dressed. A friend of mine was comfortable wearing designer suits, ties and Ferragamo shoes every day to work.

The last time I contacted him he was still employed at the high-end hotel chain and achieving his goals successfully. His current manager continues to be impressed with his professionalism and his dressing style.

In the 21st century, so many dress styles have changed over the years. No longer you should select conservative clothes while being called in for an interview.

It used to be that a woman should wear a navy suit with a white shirt and the man should wear a dark suit or a grey suit for an interview. However, if you are applying for a job in the music industry or arts, some of them wear bright colors, which is highly acceptable.

Most people in the arts or music industry wear subdued clothing while playing for a symphony or in attendance at a museum; on the other hand, while a person is performing in a park or at another venue, the dress could be subdued or bright colors.

While you are thinking about the type of job you are interviewing for, think about the culture and realize what is defined as appropriate for the interview and what is not appropriate based on the field that you are applying – whether it is in science, technology, engineering, math (STEM), law, music, arts, retail, government, or any other field that's not listed.

It's Time to Hone Your Skills

It is your time to hone your skills by practicing, practicing, and practicing in front of your friends, in front of a mirror or anywhere else you can rehearse whether you have landed the job or looking for another job. It is essential that you are working on honing your skills. The more your skills are visibly projected, the probability of being selected are greater and you are apt to land the job.

It is ideal to determine what are your strengths and weaknesses and work on being a better person in those skills.

There are so many APPS now that you can research without going to the library. For example, if you know that you can improve upon your power point skills; this is a simple task but highly needed in today's working environment. If you don't use them now, I am sure that you will find it useful in the future. Power Point has been out for quite some time and I am sure that there will be another presentation program that will be better and more efficient. If your weakness is math or composing budgetary reports, you can also take classes that could help you at home as well as incorporate these skills in your new position.

There are so many courses through continuing education or other local community colleges that could enhance your career. Methodologies are always changing constantly the way that your skills can be utilized. The basics or foundation of the courses stay the same; therefore, if you have the basic knowledge of the skills that are required to land a job, then it would be best to go to the library and check out books that will further enhance your skills. There are also various courses that are usually offered in your current place of employment. I would suggest that you take advantage of all opportunities that are offered to you free of charge first and then pursue other paid courses that you could use now and later.

If you don't have the additional skills, then it is necessary to purchase several books to learn those skills as well as seek other resources and free webinars that are available. If you are currently working a job and you are searching for another job, you could take advantage of the courses that are offered through your job. You can also seek a coach or a mentor and let this individual know what types of skills that you would like to learn. A coach or mentor will be extremely helpful for you to enhance or hone your skills.

Coaches are not free; you must invest in yourself and other skills as needed. Perform your due diligence and research the right coach for you in order to hone your skills to the best of your ability. For example, if you have been booking speaking engagement throughout various states and you were extremely successful. Don't be fooled by paying thousands of dollars on a skill that you already possess. Instead, if you are weak in e.g., marketing, then you should think about pursuing a marketing coach in order to identify more branding strategies to help your products sell. This is critical if you are in the sales field.

A list of coaches that might be of interest are: Business & Finances, Career including how to publish a book and have your work patented, marriage coaches, life, health care, etc., the list goes on.

The goal is to find the best coach that would be beneficial to you in order to improve your skills so that you will be able to showcase or hone your skills on interviews.

If you have the time to seek another stream of income, there are ways that people can do this without neglecting their regular job. Gone are the days when persons are employed at one company for twenty-five or thirty-five years at the same employer. We are in the twenty-first century and jobs have changed over the last couple of decades. For example, telework was unheard of unless one had a serious medical condition and your employer would allow you to work from home.

Now more companies are following this trend because it is proven, if you work from home, it is less stressful than being in the office, less noise and distractions. Enhance your life and your skills as much as possible to become the best person possible. If I were you, I'd seek out coaches or mentors that are reputable and not out to take your money. Some coaches charge up to $10,000. This rate is generally based on how much information that you want to receive, but it depends on the level of content that you are looking to learn and achieve.

Be sure you find out everything about what the coaching entails so that you will be able to make a prudent decision whether this is the right coach for you. Another option would be to take a couple classes in your local university to achieve the same results if possible.

You also must perform your research on this. If possible, ask to see a copy of the syllabus. This will outline the learning objectives of the course.

Coaches and mentors are similar, and the names are sometimes used interchangeably especially when the person(s) is giving you information that is helpful in an approach that you can utilize for your business or career. A coach could be a person that will guide you on a subject where you are weak in various subjects. If you don't know anything about what you are doing, then $5,000 is not an unusual price but if you have an undergraduate degree in Business, then you may be familiar with various subjects or courses that could help you.

Some of your local religious organizations and Non-religious organizations across the United States may offer courses in various skills that would possibly allow you to volunteer by offering you some of the tools necessary to travel throughout the country while learning about various cultures. In turn, this would enhance your skills and provide you with skills to gain a competitive edge over many persons competing for the same job.

This is also similar if there were several persons that are vying for the same position.

Several persons have Veteran preference and perhaps you were not in the military, but you do have the skills that would move your application to the Best Qualified List.

I am considered a mentor and I've helped many persons by assisting them to achieve their goals; however, I used to do this for years. I was not getting paid to do this. When I found out people were charging astronomical prices to do what I was doing for free, I started charging a minimum amount to assist people as to how to get a job.

I hope the information that I am providing to you is beneficial as you position yourself by absorbing the information to use to your advantage. Ultimately, I anticipate this book will help you obtain a job and perhaps you could recommend this book to other people so that they could catapult as well.

YOU HAVE LANDED THE JOB

Now that you have landed the job—you are probably saying to yourself, "What do I do next?" My answer to the question: It is necessary to keep the job that you have just landed. For those persons who have worked in a company for some years know that the adage that is typically used in a relationship, "What it took to get him or her, you have to work to keep them. This can be said in keeping the job that you have worked so hard to obtain. There is a plethora of things that you might want to consider while keeping a job once you have landed it:

While you are at work, concentrate on your projects and when they are due. This means work is not a place to socialize nor is it a place for gossiping.

Focus on deadlines and what is coming up next for you to do. Keep track of deadlines via calendar To-Do Lists that are automated.

Check in with your employees if you are in a management position to see if there is anything that you can do for them, e.g., perhaps assigned projects that need clarification—you want to ensure that you are following the guidelines for a particular project. See your manager for further clarity.

Dress in accordance with the appropriate business attire that is in congruent to the office environment. Today, that might be considered business casual for everyday and you might dress up if you are attending a very important meeting when there are people within the company and ones that are outside your company. These are your internal and external customers/stakeholders.

Don't take extended lunches unless it is approved by your management. In this case, it would be appropriate to alert management that you have to go somewhere important and there is a possibility that you might be late coming back to the office.

You have worked hard and "You Have Landed the Job," that you have worked for over the past several weeks or months preparing, and you have followed everything that is in this book and "Congratulations" are in order! I knew that if you followed all the guidelines in this book, you will land the job. It is because of your steadfastness and your tireless desire to obtain the job that you desired. You have obtained the skills that you needed. It may have been a long drawn-out process for some and for others it could have been something that was mentioned in this book that you read that gave you that "Aw Ha" moment that helped you accomplish your goals. It is all about accomplishing your goals.

By now you are working on your job and you are getting along with your fellow co-workers on your job. You have observed the culture of your job and by now you are starting to build relationships on the job. You want to build positive working relationships and it is necessary that you try to get along with everyone without being overconfident or have too much hubris. It is one thing to be confident in your skills and the way you position yourself to maintain a sense of humbleness.

You have a wealth of knowledge—don't be timid if you don't know some of the skills once you are working on the job; most people want to help you or show you how to navigate within a new job. People will look up to you if you let them know you don't know everything, but you are willing to learn from them as well. Especially, if you are in a management position, everybody wants to have a good rapport with their manager. In order to build a good relationship with your manager You must be a good listener. Remember the managers do not know it all either. Once they have had a chance to explain to you what your job is and where you will be sitting; it is okay to add some additional input about your experience and how successful projects that you managed were implemented worked for you at your previous job. Both of you need to be reciprocators. It is necessary to gain and earn respect from your managers that are above you as well as your subordinates.

It is time to get to work whatever your line or business is whether it is engineering, business, finances, arts, or music. Do the best work that you can possibly do during the time that you are employed and work on your knowledge that you have learned in your past jobs as well as the knowledge and skills that are necessary to keep a job. Attitude plays a major part in landing a job as well as maintaining your current position. Don't expect to maintain a job if the only thing you do is cause conflicts with others in the office.

As skilled and important a person may be in his/her craft, a bad attitude will totally ruin your productivity, and this could be detrimental to your new job. You can always avoid situations such as this. This might not be you but if you know that you have a problem, seek professional help. An individual may be one of the most highly intelligent on the job and is quite shrewd in finances and math; however, if he or she cannot get along with people, it might be necessary to recommend that individual(s) receive counseling.

You will lose your job every time and the company will find a way to eliminate you from your job through whatever means that are feasible for the company based on the return on investment (ROI).

A company is required to do whatever is legal and ethical in order to avoid a lawsuit as much as possible. If downsizing is a means to eliminate someone, unfortunately, this is what must happen in order to avoid frivolous lawsuits. After all, the company would want to avoid these lawsuits as much as possible. If you know of someone who has this problem and if you are friends with a similar person, I hope that you will share the reason why he or she cannot keep a job because of his or her behavior. This type of attitude is usually found in those individuals that have not worked on the job that long or immature workers that lack working with various personalities.

This also could happen to people who are seasoned or mature people and I am sure most of us know people like this. If you have co-workers like this on your job, it is highly advisable to enroll in courses or check out some books that explains "How to Deal with Difficult People." If this gets to be too difficult, you may have a conversation with your managers and let them know what is going on in the work environment and perhaps there could be a discussion to set up a training class from someone in Equal Employment Opportunities to talk with the group. It is always proactive to head off situation(s) before it becomes a major issue

Always perform research to help you improve on the job by following up with your managers and make sure they look good. If they look good, then you look good as well and then you are looked upon at work to be extremely efficient and knowledgeable. After all, it is your goal to do your job to the best of your abilities and ensure correctness and efficiency.

If you have people that you manage, it is good to set an example of the persons that work under you to ensure the same work ethics. Be sure you stay up to date on your To-Do List and other action items that are due at the designated time or several days before the deadline date is due.

How to Succeed After You Land the Job

Trying to keep a job is important as well. Don't be like some others and think that just because you get a job, you don't have to work for the job. This is a myth. Even as you have had the opportunity to be on the job six months to a year from now, it is still necessary to dress the part as well as practice good hygiene. This goes true for your teeth, including your entire body. More than likely you are interacting with people all the time and it is nothing worse than forgetting your deodorant. Just in case if you forget personal items, it is a good time to carry personal belongings in a small makeup or shaving kit for emergencies.

I have worked as a manager for a while and being in the presence of so many people daily, I have had other people tell me that a manager was hired at a well-known Health Facility working for the government and she would come in the office with her hair unkempt and unwashed on a daily basis, dress hems were coming apart and she had a foul body odor.

Her managers had to have a conversation with her about improving her attire and body odor or she would be dismissed. I don't know the full gist of the story, but I believe they ended up letting her go.

I am including these stories for situational awareness—typically, hygiene factors are taught at home or in grade school but sometimes life gets in the way that would cause a person to neglect these things, such as death of a loved one, divorce, depression, etc. We all should be cognizant of these factors and handle them accordingly. If a person can't handle these types of problems, it is wise to seek professional assistance by Contacting The Depression Hotline or Suicide Hotline.

How to Succeed After You Land the Job

One of the first thing to do if you would like to succeed on the job is to eliminate conversations that are trivial—the main subject is complaining about the manager and letting other people know your business. People can be very conniving and when it comes down to getting a promotion, you might not be the only one that is in line for the next promotion, e.g., scenario: everybody in the office knows that you dislike the boss, including persons located outside of your organization.

When people know too much of your business, e.g., Bob thinks that he is going to get a promotion but he is a gossiper that has been spreading malicious stories and fabricating information.

Suddenly, this fabrication of malicious information has gotten back to management and they are infuriated with Bob. If they thought he had a chance for management, that thought has been dismissed. A person like this can't be trusted and is labeled a busybody or a troublemaker. If you are employed by a large agency or company, there can be many. All offices have at least one or more in the office or wherever you are employed.

A person with this type of personality is not capable of being trusted in a management position, not unless the entire company is corrupt, including management. Hopefully, this is not the case. There are people that mind his/her business, always on time for work and always willing to take the extra step by learning the job as well as volunteering for more work if they have the free time, however; don't take on too much work that would not allow you to do your own work. If you do this, you are defeating the purpose. It will be your intentions of finishing important projects/work first before you take on additional duties.

You can also become a team player and pitch in for someone who doesn't have that much experience on the job or the knowledge. If you help the team member, I am sure it would be greatly appreciated, especially if the person just started the job and is not familiar with the project that needs to be done and what are the processes to complete the job. Explain to the person what needs to be done and where he/she needs to find the processes that he/she needs to follow.

This shouldn't take long; however, if the person doesn't know where various information is being stored, provide them with where to find the main calendar, supplies, processes, etc., that would help the new employee come up to speed. If you offer your services, I am sure he/she would be greatly appreciative of these services.

The only person that he/she remembers are the people that they were introduced to on the first day. We have all been there and trying to remember everybody's name is quite a challenge. For example, as a peer to the new employee, you may think that the time that you've spent with the person by showing him the ropes, would be a task that would be overlooked. Remember, no matter what you do, whether the task is large or small, management is paying attention to you because of the mere fact that you took the extra time to spend with the new employee to explain the specifics of the job.

Just so happens when you think that your task has gone unnoticed, the supervisor stops by your desk to let you know how appreciative that she was of you allowing the new employee to shadow you to show the employee the processes and procedures that would be helpful and would make the new employee improve and get a jump start in figuring out the missing pieces. A situation like this one is a win-win situation for all.

Because of what you have done by volunteering to be a mentor to the new employee it has reduced the time that would ordinarily take two to three months for the new employee to catch on but with your guidance, this has reduced the time that it took to complete the project and the project is ahead of schedule. A situation such as this could not only be recognized by the 1st line supervisor, but the 2nd level supervisor and up the chain. Although the new employee may not get recognized right away, however, 2nd level management chain could mention at the director's staff meeting how a project was about to slip and you worked with the new employee in order to help escalate the project to be ahead of schedule to avoid a schedule slippage.

Don't let the person in the next cubicle or office upset you in any way; try to maintain your composure by staying calm whenever stress is prevalent. If you feel as though you are about to lose it, take a walk to clear your head and the thoughts that you are currently having. Go to the bathroom and take some deep breaths and hold them by inhaling and exhaling. This simple little exercise will help you to eliminate the pressure that you are experiencing as well as to perform a reality check. The reality check is, e.g., I have a wife, two kids and another one on the way.

You are thinking that my wife will be going out on extended maternity leave and she will not start back to work until the baby is born and she will not start back until the baby is at least six months old. Now you are thinking logically because you do not want to lose your job after a petty incidence that happened in the office. You are saying in your mind mentally that your family needs you and the job. If he doesn't have a second income started yet, there will be medical bills along with the basic living expenses.

I would always advise anybody in a similar situation to really think about what you are doing first and do not make hasty decisions that would put yourself and your family in jeopardy. This goes the same in any given situation if you are single. If you are single, it is still just as expensive than if you had a spouse or roommate.

It is wise to save a certain percentage of your salary for unanticipated items. Unexpectant situations occur on the job all the time. This is a "what if scenario," e.g., when you first start work, another employee who was responsible for compiling the budget did not allocate enough funds for you to work for one year. After trying to strategize and borrow from other organizations; ultimately, it came down to the very end that they could only let you work for six months and they either had to borrow funds from another organization to keep you employed or terminate you. This is a hypothetical situation; however, this could be a real situation. Your first instinct would be to call your former boss and ask could you come back. On the other hand, they had already let you know that if it didn't work out, you are welcome to come back.

This would be great news for your boss being that you were an asset to the department as a whole and they depended on you to solve various problems.

In a crisis such as this it is critical to keep all doors open when you leave one place and go to another one. You always want to maintain a cordial relationship with your former employer. If a situation like this does occur, you would be prepared for unforeseen circumstances just in case you might have to go back to your last job. When most people leave, they are so anxious to leave, they don't think about the worst-case scenario. This is a situation that you have to strategize to ensure that you are making the best decision; unforeseen instances do occur, and it is best to be prepared for any situation.

After all, there is a primary reason why you were selected for the job; you have the skills, personality, and the intellect. This is a reason why it is important not to lose your cool at the workplace by getting upset. "You never know, you might have to go back."

Congratulations! You have Landed the Job!

CPSIA information can be obtained
at www.ICGtesting.com
Printed in the USA
BVHW031814160922
647215BV00011B/890